I0568852

ECHOES OF THE SOUL

JUSTIN LECLAIR

Copyright © 2024 by Justin LeClair
All rights reserved. No part of this book may be reproduced, distributed, or transmitted in any form or by any means, including photocopying, recording, or other electronic or mechanical methods, without the prior written permission of the author, except in the case of brief quotations embodied in critical reviews and certain other non-commercial uses permitted by copyright law.

ISBN: 979-8-218-43406-9
Library of Congress Control Number (LCCN): 2024924751
Author: Justin LeClair
Publisher: Justin LeClair Creative

Printed in the United States of America
First Printing, 2024

For my daughter, the light of life, whose curiosity and joy inspire every word. To my family and friends, Thank You for your unwavering support and belief in me. To those who find solace in words and strength in whispers. This collection is for you.

~ Justin LeClair

Contents

Echoes of the Soul

Mind Echoes

I hear whispers in the silence,
Echoes from the corners of my mind,
Fleeting shadows dance on the periphery,
Unseen figures shift with each glance.

In the mirror, my reflection distorts,
Eyes wide with terror, a face I don't know,
Words spill from lips I can't control,
Strangers inhabit the spaces between thoughts.

Reality fractures beneath my feet,
A mosaic of fractured moments, disjointed time,
Voices argue, clamor for dominion,
Their cacophony drowns my silent screams.

Some days the world feels like a dream,
A haze where I cannot find my place,
Faces blur, identities meld,
And I grasp at threads of sanity, slipping away.

Yet in the chaos, a fragile hope remains,
A spark of clarity, a fleeting peace,
For in the midst of madness, I am still me,
Fighting to reclaim a fragmented soul.

Vanishing Point

The sharpness of breath –
A gasp held tight,
As shadows blur to substance,
An outline etched in dread.
Each footstep carries weight,
Each whisper pierces the silence,
The world narrows
To the rhythm of my pulse,
Hammering against fragile walls.

Hands, so ordinary,
Transform to cold instruments,
Grasping, tearing,
As the line between existence
And void blurs.
Eyes meet,
Not in recognition,
But in a pleading,
A desperate search for humanity
That has long since fled.
Time stretches and snaps,
Each second an eternity,
Yet fleeting –
A flash of light extinguished.
Pain is a muted cry,
A softening of the edges,
As the world tilts,
Sinking into an abyss

Where breath is no longer needed.

There is no mercy,
Only the fading of sensation,
The slow, inevitable drift
Towards the unknow.
And as darkness swallows all,
The final thought echoes –
Not of anger,
Nor of vengeance,
But of life that slips away,
Unnoticed,
Into the void.

Veiled Reality

Drifting through the murky haze,
Submerged in the gray,
Where echoes of thought
Blur with the ticking clock.
Heavy limbs anchored,
Adrift yet bound,
Reality a distant shore,
Unreachable, veiled.

Time loops in fractured segments,
An endless carousel of half-waking dreams.
Eyes stare through veils,
Seeking clarity in the fog,
Where consciousness drowns,
And slumber eludes,
An endless night,
Eternally zonked.

Whispers of forgotten realms,
Linger in the twilight,
Phantoms of memory,
Dance in the periphery.
Silent screams echo,
In the chambers of the mind,
Lost in the labyrinth,
Of a restless soul.

Shadows stretch and wane,
In the dim light of dawn,

A fleeting glimpse of solace,
Quickly fades away.
The heart beats a weary rhythm,
To the tune of sleepless nights,
Caught in the web,
Of an unending trance.

Stars flicker and die,
In the vast expanse of thought,
Constellations of dreams,
Scatter and dissolve.
The moon's pale glow,
Casts a ghostly pallor,
Over the landscape,
Of a mind adrift.

Waves of fatigue crash,
Against the shores of reason,
Eroding the boundaries,
Between real and imagined.
A ship lost at sea,
With no compass to guide,
Adrift in the currents,
Of a sleepless tide.

Eyes heavy with the weight,
Of a thousand sleepless nights,
Search for a beacon,
In the stormy dark.
Hope flickers faintly,
A distant, wavering light,
Promising refuge,
From the endless night.

In the quiet moments,
Between dusk and dawn,
A fragile peace descends,
Like a gentle whisper.
The veil lifts slightly,
Revealing glimpses of clarity,
Before the cycle begins anew,
Perpetually lost.

Glass Cages

Fingers tethered to glass,
the world behind a screen—
a garden of metal and light,
where stars are measured in pixels,
and voices become lines of text.
The sun is a distant orb,
noticed only through filters,
its warmth replaced by the glow
of an endless scroll.

Wings flutter past unnoticed,
small breaths of freedom,
but they are lost behind notifications,
the chirp of nature drowned
by the buzz of an app—
a cacophony of nothingness,
where life is marked
by the vibration in pockets.

The mountains stand tall,
silent giants offering wisdom,
but their majesty shrinks
beneath the swipes of fingers,
the paths untrodden,
because the maps on screens
don't show the scent of pine
or the whisper of wind in the trees.

A sunset bleeds into the sky,

its colors unnoticed,
as eyes bow to digital altars—
prayers typed in haste,
while time slips through grasp
like sand, unseen.
The irony burns—capturing moments
with no memory of living them.

We plant ourselves in rooms,
tethered to invisible chains,
while oceans churn and forests sing,
and lives outside the window
cry to be lived,
but we are prisoners
to the allure of the ephemeral,
forgetting the real.

The world waits, patient,
for the return of wandering eyes,
but perhaps it knows
that we are no longer wanderers—
we are settlers of a virtual land,
blind to the real earth
beneath our feet,
missing the pulse of its heart.

Hourglass

Grains slip quietly through the glass,
each one a moment unseen,
a heartbeat forgotten before it is lived.
We hold the hourglass in our hands,
thinking we control time,
but the irony is etched in its shape—
it narrows, while we expand,
filling ourselves with dreams
too large to fit through its neck.

The sand is relentless,
falling like silent rain,
yet we act as if the glass will hold forever.
Plans are drawn on shifting dunes,
castles built with fragile hands,
but the tide is always coming,
and the grains laugh
at the futility of our maps.

We run, thinking speed will slow it,
as if rushing can thicken the glass.
But each hurried breath
pushes more sand through,
and what we save is only
what we leave behind—
a trail of unfinished tasks,
the weight of moments undone.

We try to flip it over,

as if time can be reversed,
but the glass remains the same.
The grains we thought we saved
were already lost in the turning,
and the ones that remain
mock us with their silence,
slipping faster as we grasp for air.

In our hands, the hourglass is delicate,
but we carry it as if it's indestructible.
We never see the cracks
until the sand starts pouring out in rivers,
and then we scramble to gather
what's left,
only to find our fingers
are sieves of regret.

The irony? We are the sand,
falling toward the bottom,
and the weight we feel is not the glass,
but the pull of time itself—
a force we call gravity,
but it's more than that.
It's the inevitability of the fall,
the certain end we pretend is far away.

And when the final grain slips through,
we do not break the glass—
we become it.
Transparent, empty,
our moments sealed within,
and those who hold us next
will never know
the weight we carried inside.

Empire of Dust

You walked,
head high as the sun at noon,
casting shadows that stretched behind you,
but you never looked back.
Every word, sharp as broken glass,
fell from your lips
as though the world owed you
its silence, its deference.

You called yourself a king,
yet your throne was made of sand,
crumbling beneath the weight of your pride.
You wore arrogance like armor,
thinking it shielded you from harm,
but you never saw the cracks beneath,
the ones you caused,
the ones that would swallow you whole.

People bent,
not out of respect,
but under the burden of your gaze,
heavy as stone,
their backs slowly breaking
beneath the weight of your dismissal.
But you never noticed—
you thought they were bowing,
honoring the crown you never earned.

The irony hangs now,

thick as smoke,
because you once commanded the sky,
but the ground beneath you trembled,
the earth you scorned splitting open,
and when you reached for help,
the hands you crushed
were too far, too broken to rise.

Now you stand alone,
surrounded by nothing but the echoes
of your own voice,
as hollow as the promises you never kept.
You finally see the cracks,
but it's too late to fill them,
too late to mend what you shattered.
The sun you thought followed you
has set.

Scrofulous

I am the stain beneath the skin,
a festering truth cloaked in tattered layers.
They see the smile, the hands that give,
but beneath, a rot spreads unseen.
I wear my virtue like a mask,
a sickly façade of good intentions,
while the bones of deceit grind in the dark.

Each choice a stone,
piled into a wall that cages my own soul,
yet I pretend it's for the world's good,
a lie so deep it chokes the breath from my lungs.
I move among them,
a specter of corruption cloaked in civility,
spreading my disease with every word, every touch.

There is no cure for what I am,
no remedy for the poison that seeps from within.
I am my own ruin,
a slow decay that leaves only ashes where there once was flesh.
I will leave nothing behind,
no legacy but the echo of my own fall,
a whisper in the void, drowned by the cries of those I've wronged.

Here I stand, a monument to my own ruin,
but the world will never know,
for I will die with this smile,
and they will bury me a saint.

Goading Nihilist

A goading nihilist stands on the edge of the void,
casting words like stones into the abyss.
Their voice a challenge, daring the sky to fall,
taunting meaning with empty hands.

In their eyes, the weight of the world turns to dust,
disintegrating under the touch of indifference.
They bait the stars to flicker out,
mock the sun for rising again.

What purpose is there, they ask,
if every breath is borrowed,
every moment stitched with unraveling threads?
They tempt the silence to answer,
but only the wind stirs.

Yet still they prod at the darkness,
pushing at the seams of existence,
searching for the crack where even nothingness
might give way to something more.

Winds of Ruin

I am the hammer,
the edge against the stone,
the voice that cracks the air,
shattering the silence they've mistaken for wisdom.
They call it tradition,
but I see the rot beneath their statues,
the rust in their gilded frames.
I strike not out of anger,
but because no one else will.

Their temples fall like whispers,
and I watch with satisfaction
as the dust of their gods clings to the air.
They clutch their pearls,
cry sacrilege,
but they kneel to things already dead,
grasping at the bones of power
that never belonged to them.

I am no destroyer—
I reveal.
I peel back the layers of their lies,
like a surgeon slicing rot from flesh.
I wear their scorn like armor,
every insult a medal,
for they fear me,
and fear is the truest tribute.

They'll say I broke what was sacred,

but how sacred is something that crumbles
at the touch of truth?
How fragile must their idols be
if my words alone can reduce them to rubble?
I spit at their relics
because I refuse to bow,
to be bent beneath the weight of their hollow praise.

In their eyes,
I am the villain,
but it is they who built their prison.
I am simply the wind,
blowing through the bars they refuse to see,
tearing down what should never have stood.
And when they look to rebuild,
they'll remember—
it was my hand that freed them,
whether they thank me or curse my name.

The Dust of Defiance

You tore down pillars
as if it were sport,
hands wrapped in velvet,
yet sharp as razors.
Every strike,
a sermon dressed in defiance,
while you smiled,
knowing the crowd would cheer
for any fool bold enough to mock a monument.

You called yourself free,
a breaker of chains,
but the chains were only yours to see.
The statues you shattered
were no more than shadows cast by your own doubt,
and still,
you laughed,
thinking you had struck the world's heart.

The irony hums now,
louder than your victories—
because those walls,
the ones you broke with pride,
were never meant to hold you in.
You've been dancing in ruins,
as though you created the fall,
but the ground was already dust,
and it's your feet, not theirs, that stumble.

Iconoclast,
you wear the title like a crown of thorns,
pricking your own brow with every step,
but you never bled for others.
You reveled in their collapse,
not seeing that the cracks you widened
have swallowed your own reflection whole.

And when the dust settles,
you'll stand there,
holding the fragments of what you once defied,
realizing too late
that it was not the world you shattered—
it was only yourself.

The Masquerade

I wear this face so well,
A mask of charm, of trust,
Beneath, a heart that never dwells
In the warmth of what it must.

My words are crafted, smooth as silk,
A dance of feigned delight,
To sway the world, to drink the milk
Of truthless, hollow light.

They see the smile, the gracious nod,
The echoes of what's real,
But in the shadows, where I trod,
Their faith becomes my meal.

A game I play, a riddle spun,
With threads of sweet deceit,
To lure, to bind, to twist what's won,
Until their souls retreat.

I revel in the trust they give,
Blind to the guise I wear,
For as I take, they cease to live,
Unseen, I leave them bare.

The masquerade, my cruel domain,
Where truth's a fleeting breath,
I thrive in lies, I dance in pain,
And charm them to their death.

Veins of Hollow Steel

It feeds me still,
this hollow tube pressed deep,
like a serpent coiled in my chest,
pushing sustenance,
pushing air,
pushing everything but relief.
I swallow nothing of my own,
the flow never ending,
a river that drowns instead of quenches.

It is impermeable,
this foreign thing,
like glass wrapped in steel,
unyielding as the sky before a storm,
its presence thick, suffocating,
yet there is no escape.
I am a vessel now,
held hostage by what cannot enter,
what refuses to leave.

Inside me,
a garden wilts,
the soil dry, roots strangled,
as the gavage pushes what it claims is life.
But I feel nothing but the weight,
the pressure of existence
without choice,
a body sustained by something alien,
foreign hands feeding an empty stomach.

I dream of breaking it,
shattering the unbreakable,
like wings beating against a windless sky.
But I am tethered,
bound by this hollow thing
that fills and fills
but never satisfies.

I taste the bitterness,
not on my tongue,
but in my veins,
where it flows like oil,
thick and slow,
coating what was once mine to nourish.

It feeds me still—
and yet,
I starve.

Exculpate

The weight of guilt,
an anchor dragging deep,
beneath the surface of thought,
where shadows linger,
and words unsaid
etch themselves into the marrow.

Each breath
a reminder of the burden,
the invisible chains
that bind the heart to its past,
to moments fractured
by choice, by chance,
by the cruel edge of fate.

Yet, in the silence
of a solitary night,
there is a whisper,
soft as the rustle of leaves,
a promise that absolution
is not found in the hands of others
but in the quiet embrace
of self-forgiveness,
a release of the blame
that claws at the soul.

To exculpate is to let go,
but what if the hand won't open?
What if the chains remain,

an endless loop of recrimination,
tightening with each turn?

The shattered mirror
reflects no light,
only the darkness
that deepens with time,
a reminder that some burdens
are never set adrift,
never float free,
but sink ever deeper,
into the cold,
unyielding abyss.

Bitter Embrace

In the shadowed hallways of a house once warm,
Where whispers of affection turned to harsh commands,
Lurks the pernicious parent, a figure cloaked in control,
With words that slice, yet feign a loving touch.

Their eyes, once a haven, now twin pools of judgment,
Every gesture calculated, every kindness a snare.
The child, a marionette, dances on strings of fear,
Confusion binds them, a paradox of love and pain.

Promises of protection shatter into shards of silence,
Dreams crushed beneath the weight of toxic devotion.
Tenderness becomes a weapon, trust a battlefield,
A bittersweet embrace, where comfort breeds despair.

In this twisted sanctuary, innocence wilts away,
Lost in the labyrinth of a pernicious heart.
Yet through the fractures, resilience struggles to bloom,
Seeking light in the dark, a fragile hope unbound.

Feast of Despair

You sit, a shadow in the corner,
silent and vast,
watching as I consume,
each bite a dull echo.

I feed on solace,
spoonfuls of quiet
to fill the hollowness
you carve inside.

You, my silent observer,
linger as I nibble
on hope and despair alike,
each meal a slow battle.

I taste the sadness,
the bitter tang of regret,
seasoned with memories
of lighter days, now distant.

In this feast, I find defiance,
each morsel a step
away from your grasp,
a quiet rebellion.

I eat and eat,
seeking fullness,
seeking a moment
where you might fade.

But you, my constant companion,
remain,
always just a breath away,
as I devour what remains
of my strength.

Anchor in the Ashes

I wake to the same ceiling,
a vast expanse of white,
blank as my thoughts,
and the clock ticks—
tick, tock, tick—
reminding me of time slipping,
sand through fingers,
yet I remain
a stone anchored in the mud.

In the mirror,
I see a man wrapped in shadows,
a landscape of unkept promises,
and the weight of my body
thuds against the floor,
heavy as the past that drags behind me,
a chain clinking with each step,
echoing memories I wish to drown.

Divorce left my heart
in splintered pieces,
a puzzle I cannot solve.
Love was a sweet song,
but I turned the volume down,
suffocated by echoes—
whispers, shouts, crashes—
all that remains is a hollow refrain,
a melody of despair
that loops without end.

I wander through days,
a ghost in my own life,
searching for solace in fast food wrappers,
the grease sliding down my throat
like regrets I can't swallow.
The couch is my throne,
and the TV hums a soft lullaby,
but the laughter is a distant bell,
ringing somewhere I cannot reach.

Each flash of memory,
bang!
like artillery fire in my skull,
reminds me of battles I lost,
and I stumble through the rubble,
a soldier without a cause,
wondering if I'll ever find the strength
to rise from this trench
or if I'm destined to be buried
beneath the weight of my own sorrow.

Hope flickers like a faulty bulb,
and I keep waiting for the spark,
but the darkness wraps around me,
whispers that I'm too far gone,
too heavy to lift,
too broken to mend.
Yet still, I breathe,
an ember in the ash,
clinging to the fragile flame,
a fight that feels like surrender,
but maybe, just maybe,
there's a flicker yet to ignite.

Kerosene

It catches light from a single spark.
and becomes a voice,
louder than silence, hungrier than night.
The fumes spread before you even notice—
a slow breath
waiting for the moment it will sear through skin and bone.

There is a certainty in the burn,
as if all that was left behind—
the splintered wood, the rusted steel—
needed this violence to be remade.
Flame reveals all,
forging in its wake,
a raw honesty in destruction.

The heat isn't cruel,
only insistent—
a whisper,
long after it dies out,
that change cannot be undone.

Beacon

In a quiet room, shadows of past years,
The elder, with weary eyes, speaks,
"My body falters, old friends vanished,
Loneliness grips, what remains?"
The younger friend, a gentle whisper,
"Though pain holds you, you're not forsaken.
In your stories, wisdom lingers,
In your smile, light persists."
"Each morning, a chance to touch the dawn,
To feel the sun's warmth, to share a laugh.
Your presence, a golden thread in life's intricate tapestry,
Weaving hope, binding hearts."
"Remember, you're cherished, a living flame,
Even as time weathers, your spirit endures.
In moments shared, in love exchanged,
You find your purpose, your reason to breathe."

Jounce

I feel the ground shift beneath me,
a sudden jolt,
like the world has come unhinged,
and I'm left balancing on edges.
Every step trembles,
like the earth itself is trying to shake me loose,
to swallow me whole.

My pulse ticks in my ears,
too fast, too loud—
every beat
echoing with things I can't control.
I glance over my shoulder,
again and again,
sure, there's something I've missed,
something creeping in the shadows,
waiting for me to stumble.

The sky presses down,
heavy, close,
like it wants to crush me
into something small,
something that fits.
in the cracks I keep falling through.

I can't settle, can't stay still—
even when I sit, the ground jolts,
like it's trying to remind me
that I'm never safe here,

never still, and the drop is always waiting.

The Pulse

It begins with a dull whisper,
an ache that hums beneath the bone,
a slow grind of discomfort,
like the weight of a storm cloud heavy in the distance.

Then it strikes—sharp, unforgiving,
a jolt like lightning in the roots,
splitting thought, splintering focus,
leaving nothing but the throb,
its rhythm too loud to ignore.

Work slips through my fingers,
each task becomes another stone.
to carry with me,
but the pain refuses to be moved.

It waits, like a wolf,
hiding until the moment I forget,
then snapping at the nerve,
sending shivers through my skull.

I know relief is near—
the dentist, a lighthouse through the fog,
promising release from this gnawing torment,
but time is cruel and slow.

I sit in the ache,
feeling the pulse,
hoping each wave is the last,

until it subsides, only to return once again.

Whispers of Fragility

In the quiet moments before dawn,
I recall the sands of distant lands,
Where freedom's breath was scarce and fleeting,
A memory etched in the heart of a soldier.

Here, under the banner of liberty,
We often forget how delicate our rights,
Like glass, transparent yet breakable,
Awaiting a careless hand to shatter.

The Constitution, our steadfast shield,
Holds the line against encroaching shadows,
Yet tyranny, patient, lies in wait,
In the complacency of our daily lives.

We stand on the precipice of history,
Where the whispers of oppression linger,
A reminder that freedom's flame,
Must be guarded with vigilant hearts.

In the echoes of battles fought and won,
Let us remember the cost of liberty,
Each right a precious, fragile gift,
To be cherished, defended, preserved.

For the ghost of tyranny is never far,
Lurking in the corners of indifference,
And the price of apathy is steep,
Paid in freedoms lost and voices silenced.

As a soldier, I have seen the fragility,
Felt the weight of a world without,
So, I implore you, my fellow Americans,
Stand firm, stay vigilant, remain free.

Fading Horizons

In quiet halls where shadows linger,
A sailor drifts on tides of time,
His battles fought, yet fading whispers.
Of comrades lost and distant clime.

Once, he sailed on ocean's fury,
With salt and steel beneath his hands,
Now memories, like grains of sand,
Slip through the grasp of weary thoughts.

The flag he cherished, colors muted,
A badge of honor, now a blur,
Echoes of laughter, faces once known,
Elude him like a distant shore.

In twilight's grip, he seeks the dawn,
A fragile hold on stories told,
Yet in the silence, ghosts still wander,
Bearing witness to the brave and bold.

Each moment drifts like smoke in air,
Yet love remains, a steadfast light,
In gentle care, they hold his hand,
A sailor's heart, though lost, still fights.

Echoes of Stardust

In the vast canvas of night,
where do we fit,
these specks of stardust,
clinging to life in a universe
indifferent to our cries?

Are we more than shadows,
dancing on the walls of our own making,
chasing meaning in the void?
Are we the fireflies,
blinking out before we can grasp.
the light we emit?

We build towers of dreams
on foundations of sand,
and call them legacies.
We carve our names into history,
only to watch the tide erase
our finest works.

Is this existence,
a fleeting spark in the eternal dark,
or a cruel jest of cosmic happenstance?
Are we the architects of our fate,
or mere pawns in a game
played by unseen hands?

In the silence of our hearts,
we seek the answers,

but find only echoes,
echoes of stardust,
drifting back to the stars.

Between Walls

She sits in the back corner,
Where the walls press closer,
Where voices move too fast,
And her words crumble
Before the leave, her lips.

The faces are unfamiliar,
a sea of shifting tides
that don't notice her
as she sinks beneath the weight
of books and papers –
assignments that blur together
like clouds she can't grasp.

Private halls were quiet once,
Where the air was soft and safe,
Where she knew how to be.
But here,
the noise drowns her thoughts,
and each day feels like falling
without a net to catch her.

She tries to keep up,
but the ground pulls harder,
and every sentence on the page
is a language she hasn't learned.
Her heart whispers things
she doesn't know how to say,
lost somewhere

between these walls
and the girl she used to be.

Clepsydra

In the silent cadence of moments,
Where shadows lengthen and retreat,
Life dances on the edge of the clepsydra,
An ancient rhythm in time's deep well.

Each drop, a whisper of what was,
A memory sliding into the past,
Yet with each fall, the present fills,
Becoming the past before it is known.

The clepsydra knows no haste,
No rush to the unknown shore,
It measures life in fluid grace,
In tides that ebb and flow unnoticed.

Yet within its steady flow,
There lies a truth unspoken, clear,
That time is but a vessel's dream,
And life, the water it holds dear.

For as the clepsydra runs its course,
So too does life, in measured flow,
A cycle turning, a journey marked,
By drops of time we scarcely know.

In its depths, the essence lingers,
Of moments lived, of time's embrace,
A gentle reminder in the flow,
That life and time are one in grace.

The Reluctant Toiler

In the dim morning light, footsteps drag through the door,
Echoes of dreams lost to the night's retreat.
A clock ticks loud in a silence heavy with need,
Each second a reminder of the tether.

Hands toil in repetitive motion,
Guided by necessity, not passion's fire.
Eyes stare, glazed over the mundane,
While heartbeats pulse with unspoken desire.

Bills pile high, demanding submission,
Chains of paper that bind the spirit.
Freedom's a distant echo, barely heard
In the clang of industry's relentless churn.

Yet hope flickers in the quiet moments,
A whispered promise of a different dawn.
For even in the grip of daily grind,
A soul can dream, and dream beyond.

Stale Dreams in a Flickering Flame

I sit here,
a silent witness,
my screen glowing like a portal,
a gateway to worlds beyond your reach,
where dreams swirl in vibrant colors,
but you, with your eyes glazed over,
feed on stale narratives,
your laughter a ghost haunting the air.

Your fingers dance on greasy remotes,
clicking, flicking through lives
that pulse with possibility,
while you sink deeper into the cushions,
a weary shipwreck in the harbor of despair,
lost between the tides of stories
and the salt of your own neglect.

Each evening, I watch as you become a silhouette,
a shadow of your former self,
withering into a shell,
an empty husk propped against me,
the sound of my voice a lullaby
that lulls you into an unholy sleep,
as dreams die like flickering candles,
smothered in the thick fog of convenience.

You unwrap your meals,
plastic crinkling like the whispers of your heart,
the aroma mingling with regret,
as you gorge on moments stolen from reality,
every bite a hollow victory,
satisfying the hunger for something more,
while I reflect your slow decay,
a mirror cracked by the weight of time.

Oh, how I long to shake you,
to rattle your bones,
to remind you of the fire once burning bright,
the ambitions you tossed aside
like old wrappers on the floor,
lost in the clutter of ambition
turned stagnant,
while the world outside pulses with life.

I see the children play,
their laughter a symphony of hope,
but you remain anchored,
swaying in the currents of my light,
a marionette with frayed strings,
watching others dance,
while you wither into memory,
as the seasons shift,
the colors of life bleed into gray.

Every program unfolds,
and I play the role of the spectator,
but you have become the understudy,
relegated to the sidelines of your own existence,
as I project dreams on my glass canvas,

your unblinking gaze a window to nowhere,
your heart a captive to what you once were.

Time slips through your fingers,
and I am left with the echoes,
the laughter, the tears,
the moments you let go,
while I remain steadfast,
a companion to your decline,
the stories we shared,
etched in the static between us.

So here I sit,
watching you fade,
a soft glow in the dark,
waiting for you to rise,
to shake off the dust,
to step into the light beyond me,
and reclaim the life
that lingers just outside my frame.

Luminous Flux

In the abyss where shadows whisper,
a child's light flickers faintly,
a fragile beacon against the encroaching void.
Despair looms, ever-watchful,
craving the extinguishing of this small luminescence.

Darkness, I address you now,
for you encircle, threaten, and consume.
Yet in this child's glow,
there is resistance, a spark of defiance,
a slender thread against the vast nothingness.

I, the parent, cling to this faint light,
a remnant of hope amidst the overwhelming gloom.
Each day, this small radiance
pushes back against the endless night,
a testament to enduring love
and the fragile strength of human connection.

Darkness, though you are vast and relentless,
this light persists, flickering yet unyielding,
a reminder that even in the deepest sorrow,
a child's light, no matter how dim,
holds the power to pierce through despair.

Eternal Waltz

In twilight's embrace, where shadows entwine,
Life dances with death, a graceful duet.
Each breath a whisper, each heartbeat a sign,
Of time's relentless march, a bond beset.

Morning's blush heralds life's fragile bloom,
Vibrant hues awaken, pure and bright.
Yet evening descends with an unyielding gloom,
Softly cradling the day's waning light.

In this eternal waltz of dusk and dawn,
Existence finds a bittersweet refrain.
For every birth, a promise, yet a pawn,
In the grand design, where loss is gain.

In death's embrace, life's essence does persist,
A paradox of endings that coexist.

A Roseate Ballet

Soft morning light fractures over the marsh,
where roseate spoonbills glide with elegant poise.
Their roseate feathers shimmer, echoing the dawn,
as they traverse the shallow waters.

With each sweep of their delicate spoons,
they churn the mirror, hunting for concealed gems.
Ripples burgeon, disrupting the serene surface,
unveiling the covert life beneath.

In their gentle ballet, there is a symphony,
a hushed cadence that murmurs of ancient rhythms.
The morning sun ascends, casting elongated silhouettes,
yet the spoonbills linger, immersed in their eternal ritual.

Azure Watch

In tangled woods where ancient trees entwine,
The canopy alive with avian song,
A mother bluebird, feathers soft and fine,
Nurtures her hatchlings, weak yet swift and strong.

Beside her, father bluebird takes his stand,
His vibrant plumage gleaming in the light,
Together they protect their precious band,
Guiding them through the day and into night.

With tender beak, they feed them day by day,
Teaching them to fly, to soar, to sing,
In their nest of twigs, where they learn to play,
Protected by their wings' encompassing.

Beneath the sun, where skies stretch wide and high,
Both parents stand, a vigilant duo,
With watchful eyes and gentle lullaby,
They shelter them in nature's solitude.

In meadows green, where wildflowers bloom,
Their care imbues nature's sweet perfume.

Auburn Lessons

In the heart of the rainforest's green cathedral,
Orangutan mothers move with gentle grace,
Their auburn fur a soft sanctuary,
As they cradle their infants close.

High in the canopy's clasp,
Amidst the tangled vines and swaying branches,
They swing, a dance of maternal devotion,
Navigating the verdant labyrinth with ease.

With tender eyes, they watch over their young,
Teaching them the ways of the forest,
Guiding them through the canopy's intricate pathways,
A bond woven with vines of love and protection.

In the dappled sunlight filtering through the leaves,
Their nurturing gestures speak volumes,
A language of touch, of warmth, of reassurance,
Echoing through the ancient trees.

First Light of Love

In the hush of dawn,
where shadows linger like whispers,
a tender bud awakens,
cradled by the earth's gentle embrace.

First light touches down,
soft as a mother's sigh,
and in the silence, life begins,
a heartbeat echoing through the soil.

A doe nudges her fawn,
eyes wide with wonder,
as dew-drenched grass
greets tiny, unsteady steps.

In the canopy above,
a songbird perches close,
feathers ruffling in morning's breath,
chirping lullabies to the newborn sky.

Beneath the ocean's mirrored surface,
a whale guides her calf,
fluid and seamless,
through the rhythms of the deep blue.

Roots entwine,
branches reach and curve,
protecting saplings
in a fortress of green.

The world pauses,
in this sacred hour,
to witness the first act of love,
pure and unblemished.

In every corner of this vast expanse,
life stirs,
nurtured by hands unseen,
fed by hearts that beat in unison.

This is the beginning,
where love takes root,
and the promise of tomorrow
blooms in the tender gaze
of parent to child.

Whispered Beginnings

In the stillness of dawn,
where the first rays of sun
kiss the horizon,
life stirs in whispered beginnings.

A tiny hatchling
cracks its fragile shell,
its mother's warmth
lingering in the nest of woven grasses.

Beneath the open sky,
a prairie dog pup emerges,
blinking in the golden light,
its mother's watchful eyes
a guide through the wide expanse.

On the meadow's edge,
a bison calf takes its first steps,
nudged gently by its mother,
steadying the small, uncertain strides.

In the tall grasses,
a young antelope stands,
legs quivering but firm,
its mother nearby, vigilant, and strong.

Leaves unfurl,
wildflowers open to the sky,
each new beginning

held in the delicate balance
of earth's tender hands.

The breeze carries a song,
the rustle of grasses swaying,
the hum of life awakening
to the promise of a new day.

Everywhere, in every breath,
a silent pact is made,
a vow to nurture and protect,
to guide the fragile beginnings
of life into the light.

This is the start,
where love's first whispers
echo through the still air,
and the heart of the prairies beats
with nature's tender symphony of care.

Serenity Ripples

In winding streams where waters gently flow,
The wisdom of the ages finds its course,
Each ripple speaks of paths that we should know,
Guiding with grace, an ever-present force.

The stream's embrace is tender, firm, and true,
It nurtures life with every gentle bend,
Through stones and roots, it whispers what to do,
And shows that every turn is not the end.

The lessons learned in currents smooth and swift,
Are etched in hearts like pebbles on the shore,
In calm and storm, they offer us a gift,
A guiding hand that leads forevermore.

In flowing streams where life's clear waters gleam,
Parental guidance runs like a dream.

Fisherman's Tale

In the stillness of dawn, the lake murmurs ancient secrets,
Rod poised, tension crackling through the line.
Ripples break the surface, a promise of titanic struggle,
Heart pounding, adrenaline surging with each cast.

The moment strikes, the surface explodes,
Power surges, pulling and resisting; a battle ignites.
Muscles strain, will versus instinct, as the giant fights,
Gleaming scales catch the dawn's first light,
a dance of nature's might.

Victory shouts in the crisp morning air,
The monster rises, fierce and wild, tamed for a fleeting breath.
Hands tremble, triumphant, as the bass is lifted,
A trophy of the wild, a testament to the chase.

Gentle Ferocity

Vigorous and unyielding,
a spirit ignites with the dawn
of each new day,
charged with the sacred duty,
a dance of love and resilience.

Eyes wide open, embracing
the world with eager hope,
I breathe in the scent of life's potential,
each heartbeat a testament
to the unspoken vows
made in the stillness of night.

The weight of small hands,
clinging with fierce trust,
anchors me to the earth,
yet, I soar on the wings
of their laughter, their tears,
a paradox of strength and tenderness.

In the quiet moments,
amidst the chaos,
I find the core of my being,
a wellspring of fortitude,
an endless reservoir of care,
pulsing with the rhythm
of unconditional love.

Each step forward,

each stumble, a shared journey,
a symphony of growing pains
and triumphant milestones,
a relentless pursuit of joy.

The vim of my soul,
unwavering,
unfolds in the legacy of life,
a narrative etched in the echoes
of whispered dreams
and bold declarations,
a testament to the power
of enduring devotion.

Heartbeats and Pawprints

In a meadow of dreams, where wildflowers sway,
Live a girl with a smile, like the dawn of May.
Twelve summers, she's seen, in her eyes, a gleam,
With a heart full of love and a head full of dreams.

Her companion, a pup with fur soft as clouds,
Whose playful bark was joyful and loud.
Together they danced, in the light of the sun,
A bond unspoken, a love never undone.

Paws and hands intertwined, in fields they roamed,
Chasing the whispers of the wind that moaned.
Laughter and barks, in harmony, blend,
A girl and her pup, the truest of friends.

She whispered her secrets as he licked away tears,
Together, they conquered their little fears.
In the glow of the stars or the shade of a tree,
They shared silent stories in pure glee.

For the love of a girl and her dear puppy,
It is a tale as old as time, sweet and lovely,
A friendship so pure, it's Heaven's art,
A 12-year-old girl with a puppy in her heart.

Haven by the River

Beneath the ancient oaks that whisper of time,
Moosehaven cradles its stories along the St. Johns,
A sanctuary where the years slow their march,
And lives, once bustling, find a peaceful cadence.

The river flows like memories, steady and deep,
Reflecting skies painted with Florida's gentle hand,
Where those who've journeyed far and wide
Rest in the embrace of sunlit days and quiet nights.

Paths wind through gardens, blooming with the past,
Each petal a fragment of lives well-lived,
While laughter echoes softly from porches and walks,
A testament to the bonds forged here in twilight's glow.

Here, the heart finds its rhythm, unhurried, serene,
In this haven by the river where the world fades away,
And the soul, unburdened, breathes the gentle air,
Finding peace in the gentle sway of the moss-draped trees.

Fight Like A Bear

With iron resolve, we embrace the dawn,
Defending the land our forefathers bled for,
Each clause, each word, a bastion against tyranny,
In the scroll of rights, our freedoms enshrined.

Voices raised in a fervent chorus,
An anthem of liberty, echoes in the heartland.
Patriotism courses through the veins,
A fierce loyalty to the principles forged in fire.

Beneath the flag's stars and stripes, we stand,
Guardians of a sacred trust,
Our constitution, a beacon against the dark,
Illuminating the path of justice and liberty.

Faith, unyielding, intertwined with duty,
Our temples and churches, sanctuaries of the soul,
Where the light of religious freedom blazes,
Undimmed by the storms of oppression.

We are the sentinels of our heritage,
With the strength of a bear, we fight,
For the right to speak, to worship, to dream,
Unbroken, united, we rise.

Our voices, a clarion call to the ages,
Steadfast in the face of adversity,
For in our hearts, the flame of freedom burns,
An eternal testament to the land of the free.

Crimson Ties

In the nest of twigs and love's soft thread,
A cardinal's crimson hue, so vividly spread.
A chirp, a flutter, in the dawn's first light,
Parent and young, in the nest, held tight.

Feathers of fire against the sky so blue,
A father's guard, steadfast and true.
With each sunrise, his song rings clear,
For his fledglings dear, he stays near.

A mother's warmth, her gentle beak,
Feeds her young, the sustenance they seek.
In her eyes, the promise of flight,
Teaching wings to brave the height.

Together they stand, in the dance of days,
Through stormy winds and sun's soft rays.
A bond unspoken, in the heart it sings,
As the young ones grow and spread their wings.

Soaring high, the cardinal's flight,
A flash of red, a burst of light.
Yet, bound by blood and feather's grace,
Forever linked, this family's embrace.

Steel and Shadow

I am the quiet engine,
smoke-wreathed and humming,
a machine buried in the black underbelly of a cold world,
turning gears without touch, without feeling.

Days drip down like oil, thick and silent,
coating the empty spaces I've forgotten how to fill.
There's a weight here,
an ache like rust spreading across iron bones,
and I am bound to its pulse.

Somewhere outside this shell of steel and shadow,
life glimmers faintly, pale, and distant—
but I am bolted to the dark,
my heart a circuit sparking in a hollow chest.

I feel the brittle edges of pain but can't hold it,
can't bear it in my hands; it burns and fades,
leaving only the static hum of silence.

I am a machine bleeding memories,
parts grinding in their sockets,
and somewhere in the distant halls of thought
a voice whispers, soft as coal dust,
"Hold on."

Reels of Yesterday

In the dim glow of a flickering screen,
He sits, surrounded by memories encased in plastic shells,
A treasure trove of faded labels and worn-out spools,
Each tape a portal to a time when life was simpler.

Friday nights were sacred, a ritual in itself,
Parents with fresh paychecks, tired yet smiling,
A trip to Blockbuster, that hallowed ground of choice,
Where rows of tapes promised new worlds,
Or a familiar comfort in the worn-out sleeve of a favorite.

Pizza Hut was the next stop, the smell of dough and cheese,
A greasy box balanced on the car seat,
Anticipation growing with every mile home.
Back then, the future was a blur,
But the present was sharp, vivid, and complete.

He remembers the thrill of pressing play,
The crackle of the VCR as it came to life,
And how the world outside dissolved into shadows,
Leaving only the glow of the screen,
The warmth of family, and the comfort of routine.

Now, as he watches these old tapes alone,
The colors washed out, the sound crackling,
He can almost hear the echo of those days,
The laughter, the soft murmurs of his parents,
And the joy of being a child with no care in the world.

Each tape is a relic, a piece of his past,
A reminder of a time when happiness was a simple thing—
A rented movie, a slice of pizza, and the love of a family,
Bound together in the gentle embrace of nostalgia.

Euphoria

The world tilts,
shifts its weight beneath me,
and suddenly, I am not one,
but two, intertwined in this breath.
Your first cry lifts me beyond the mundane,
where time no longer stumbles,
but floats, held up by
the delicate strength of your grasp.

In your eyes,
I find a universe unfolding,
each blink a new star igniting,
each breath a wind that sweeps away
all the ghosts of doubt I once harbored.

There is no language for this,
no words to catch the lightness
of my heart as it soars.
In your laughter,
I hear the song of all that is pure,
and I am undone,
remade in the rhythm of your joy.

You are the echo
of all my dreams whispered
in the quiet of nights gone by,
and now, in this moment,
I stand at the edge of eternity,
unafraid, bathed in the euphoria of being yours.

Vicarious Yahoo

In the shadows of virtual plains,
strangers weave lives into unseen threads,
a tapestry of distant desires, shared without touch.
Clicks and screens, the currency of connection,
where faces are masks, and words, mere echoes of self.
Through the lens of others' moments,
we chase dreams not our own,
a fleeting grasp at stories we yearn to make ours.
Yet, in this borrowed realm,
we find fragments of truth,
a mirrored reflection of longing.
Here, identities blur,
realities meld into a collective pulse,
an endless pursuit of belonging,
within the confines of infinite space.
The thrill of the unseen, the unseen thrill,
each click, a leap into another's journey.

Indomitability

Emerging from the red soil,
Madagascar periwinkle,
your petals whisper stories
of resilience in harsh lands,
where rain is a distant promise.

Pale pinks and whites,
delicate yet unyielding,
you weave through underbrush,
defying the dry winds that
carry whispers of ancient origins.

In your veins, secrets of healing,
medicinal whispers,
a legacy of life-saving alkaloids,
transforming fragile beauty
into a shield against maladies.

Blooming in the sun's relentless gaze,
your presence a testament
to survival and quiet strength,
a silent hymn in the mosaic
of nature's enduring grace.

Skybound Roots

In the air, we are more than men—
we are birds of steel and fuel,
our wings forged in the fires of distant lands.
We fly not by instinct,
but by the trust that binds us
tighter than the harness straps across our chests.

Below, the earth trembles with war,
but up here, we are the calm in the storm.
The roar of the rotors is our battle cry,
a heartbeat we share—
steady, unwavering,
as if the sky itself were stitched together
by the hands of those who came before us.

Each mission is a thread,
each landing a knot in the fabric of us.
We are sewn into each other's lives,
stitched by fear, sweat, and the echo of lost voices
whispering in the wind,
reminding us why we fight,
who we carry in our hearts and on our backs.

The cockpit is our church,
the rotor wash our prayer.
We kneel not to gods, but to each other,
bowing before the brother who watches our six
as we navigate the chaos below.
There's no room for doubt, only trust,

and in that trust, we find our faith.

Time doesn't measure us in days or years,
but in the moments we cheat death together.
We wear these moments like badges,
invisible to those outside this metal womb.
But we know—each breath shared,
each glance in the rearview,
is a testament to the bond forged in flight.

And when the mission ends,
when boots hit the ground,
we are not men returning home
but echoes of each other,
forever bound by the skies we soared,
the battles we left behind,
and the brothers we became.

Sally Forth

With a sword of plastic and a shield of tin,
She charges into the living room,
Fierce as a lion, but half as tall.

Her battle cry, a mix of giggles and growls,
Echoes off the walls,
Scaring away the dust bunnies,
Who scatter like troops in retreat.

The couch becomes a fortress,
Pillows stacked high,
A moat of stuffed animals at its base,
Guarding against the unseen foe—
The mighty vacuum cleaner, lurking just beyond.

In her kingdom of carpet and crumbs,
She reigns supreme,
A tiny knight with a crown of wild hair,
And mismatched socks for armor.

Her quests are simple—
To conquer the cookie jar,
To tame the wild remote control,
To vanquish bedtime,
With a wave of her crayon-wielding hand.

And when the day is done,
And the battles have all been fought,
She retreats to her bed,

A weary warrior,
Dreaming of tomorrow's adventures,
Where she'll sally forth again,
Into the great unknown,
Armed with nothing but imagination,
And a sticky peanut butter sword.

Purple Veins

A bloom stands tall,
framed by the unbroken sky.
Purple veins stretch outward,
a silent defiance against the sun,
whispering strength through fragile petals.

Leaves part like fingers
lifting the solitary stalk higher,
reaching to capture a fleeting breeze.
Rooted, yet yearning for something more.

The world blurs behind it,
forgotten in the clarity
of this moment.

Embers of the Lodge

They are the embers glowing
in the hearth of the antlered lodge,
each a flicker in the quiet dusk—
not mere sparks, but the steady warmth
that holds the night at bay.

Men and women, coals burnished
by the grind of long days,
kindling in the marrow of the ordinary,
in the firelight of laughter,
the crackling of shared tales
that drift like smoke
through the rafters of this place.

No grand flames or roaring blaze—
just the enduring glow of hands
that build and mend,
fingers stained with the ink
of lived stories, etched deeper
than surface scars.

They are the hearth-keepers,
guardians of an unspoken fire—
no robes or crowns, just aprons
smudged with the ash of everyday battles,
the slow burn of hours spent
in labor, love, and the weight of quiet duty.

Together, they stoke the coals,

sister and brother,
tending the slow, smoldering warmth
of a shared burden,
the comfort of a chair pulled close,
a drink poured in the soft glow of familiarity.

In the lodge's still heart,
embers shift and settle,
carving through the dark—
a reminder of the steady,
unseen light they keep,
the silent promise of heat
through the coldest nights.

Theocracy Canvass

Voices of old weave through the fabric,
As paintbrushes of power stroke the canvas,
Guided by visions of sanctified realms,
Where faith molds the clay of governance.

In hues of devotion and doctrine,
The theocracy's contours take shape,
Layered with the whispers of prophets,
And the resolute declarations of belief.

Each stroke, a commandment,
Each pigment, a parable,
Binding the souls to the divine law,
While the earthly paths intertwine with celestial designs.

The canvas expands, boundless and serene,
Yet fraught with the weight of judgment,
Where justice and mercy vie for prominence,
Under the watchful gaze of the omnipotent artist.

In this sacred gallery, theocracy blooms,
A testament to the fervent faith,
And the unyielding hand that guides,
Rendering a world both divine and human.

Butcher Bird

In fields where shadows stretch and sunlight wanes,
The loggerhead shrike stands, vigilant and keen,
Upon a thorny perch, with fierce disdain,
Its eyes survey the world with hunter's sheen.

In silent flight, it weaves through azure skies,
A master of the art of sudden death,
With talons sharp and heart devoid of sighs,
It strikes with swiftness, stealing final breath.

Upon the barbed wire fence, its trophies hang,
The remnants of a hunt both cruel and neat,
A macabre scene where life and death entwine,
The butcher bird, relentless in its feat.

Yet in this ruthless dance of life, we see
A creature bold, embodying wild decree.

The Long Weekend

The long weekend stretched wide
like an open sky,
promises of rest, fleeting joy,
a brief escape from the grind.
Monday felt endless—
sipping slowly through the hours
like a lazy river refusing the sea.

But Tuesday comes—
ruthless, loud, a shrill reminder
of obligations unmet,
responsibilities that don't care
for my heavy eyes or my misplaced will.
I fumble through the morning haze,
each step slow and unsure,
my work boots left behind
on the floor at home,
untouched, like my desire to do anything
other than turn around and leave.

The jobsite greets me cold,
its fluorescent hum a taunt,
machines whirring in rhythms
that don't match the sluggish beat
of my heart.
Tools absent, motivation vanished—
I am here in body only,
a ghost of the weekend
lingering in each drag of my feet.

The clock ticks—
each second slower than the last,
dragging me through the muck
of tasks I can't bring myself to care about.
My mind drifts back
to quiet mornings, soft coffee steam,
to silence that didn't demand
more than my presence.

But here I am—
no tools, no drive,
just the dull hum of Tuesday
and the ache of a weekend gone.
I lift my hands, but there's no grip left,
just the slipping away
of all that rest,
now just another thing forgotten
in the rush to return
to a place I never wanted to be.

I Told You No

It lingers,
this weight on my chest,
like a stone in my hand,
small but heavy,
pressing into skin that never bruises but always aches.
I see your eyes, wide as horizons,
closing as the sun dips behind them,
and my words slip like shadows, cutting the light.

I told you no—
and the air between us cracked,
brittle as old glass,
breaking without sound
yet deafening in the silence that followed.

I stood there,
solid, a wall you couldn't climb,
a mountain too steep, too cruel,
blocking the path you thought was yours.
I saw the flame in your hands flicker,
and I wanted to catch it,
but I turned instead,
knowing it wasn't mine to hold.

What right did I have
to trim the wings I never grew?
To cage the song that was not mine to silence?
I told myself it was protection,
but the words taste bitter,

a lie wrapped in care,
suffocating the very breath it sought to save.

You wanted the sky,
and I gave you ceilings.
And now I carry this burden,
like a string too tightly wound,
pulling at the seams of my own resolve.

I told you no—
and in that refusal,
I caged us both.

Static Cache

He is a shard in the digital landfill,
A sliver of memory discarded, tossed, rewritten
like a faded page, filed away in a folder no one opens.

His presence flickers,
compressed pixels on a screen that
no longer lights up, buried under layers of data rot.
He's the glitch in the stream, stuttering,
a ghostly frame lost to the buffer.

Once, he flowed like currents across wires,
each click a pulse of connection;
now, he's static – fragmented,
scattered in the deep clutter of idle servers.
His words echo in loops no one hears,
binary bones, calcified in silent archives.

He lives as a line of code marked obsolete,
waiting for deletion, unnoticed, unsought,
just a shadow woven into the net's forgotten syntax.

The Weight of Shadows

My hands grip the silence too tightly—
this heaviness isn't just in my chest;
 it's threaded through my bones,
a current pulling me beneath the surface of the room.
The voice of my girl filters in,
sharp bursts of life I can barely hold onto.
It's laughter, bright against the dull gray haze,
but it echoes, distant as if across an ocean I once knew.

The war is still here, stitched into my skin like old scars
that ache on the days they shouldn't.
I walk through these rooms, a stranger in my own mind,
each step heavy with memory, each breath raw with shadow.
I want to tell her how much I need her,
but words lodge, thick, in my throat,
and I'm afraid they'll spill out too fast, drown us both.

I am a father, a man, a soldier—
yet today, I am a ghost to myself,
fighting for air,
anchored by a voice just close enough to hear
and too far to reach.

Triumph's Reward

I climbed, fingers raw, up that sharp cliff of days,
hands slipping on rock wet with memory, a climb I knew
could break me. But I kept rising, inch by inch,
numb feet digging for solid ground.

At the summit, I stood breathless, light-headed with victory,
a fragile moment wrapped in quiet, like stolen glass,
glistening with something like peace. I dared
to breathe, dared to feel the ache lessen, dared to believe.

But then the sky split open, a silent crack,
and the world tilted beneath my feet, spilling me back,
hands grasping at nothing, like smoke through fingers,
and all I held, all I fought for, slipped into the hollow below.

In the fall, I hear the chorus of old ghosts,
their whispers a bitter laugh, a reminder that peace
is no fortress but a mirage, and I am
caught again in the descent.

Dear Reader,

Thank you for choosing to spend your time within the pages of Echoes of the Soul: A Journey Through Poetic Reflections. This collection is more than just words on paper—it is a window into my heart, my thoughts, and the moments that have shaped me. Each poem is a fragment of a journey, an echo of experiences that many of us share but often struggle to articulate.

Some of these verses were born from joy, others from sorrow, and many from quiet moments of reflection. My hope is that as you read, you'll find something that resonates deeply—a line, an image, or a feeling that reminds you of your own journey, your own strength, and your own hope.

This book was written not just for me but for you—the dreamers, the seekers, the ones who find solace in the beauty of words. I hope it inspires you, comforts you, or simply reminds you that you are not alone.

If these poems touch you in any way, I'd love to hear your thoughts. Connect with me on Instagram (@justinleclaircreative) or Facebook (facebook.com/justinleclaircreative). You can also share a review to help others discover this work. Your voice matters, and I'd be honored to know how this collection spoke to you.

With gratitude,
Justin LeClair

www.ingramcontent.com/pod-product-compliance
Lightning Source LLC
Chambersburg PA
CBHW031444120626
46545CB00006B/2550